This book belongs to:

_____

ISBN 978-1-7383409-3-4

I hope you will enjoy the journey of orange and mango as much as I do.

Mrs. Natalie

www.travelteacher.ca

Ever wonder how your favorite fruits land at the local supermarkets? Follow along with the journey of mango and orange today.

Wow, A book about mango & orange. YUM. My favorite fruits.

MANGOES
Chapter 1

Hello. I am Mrs. Natalie. The first part of this book we will talk about mangoes. This will be in 2 parts. We need to start at the mango orchard. Let's go!

Giving Credit:

So, a special thanks to the Mohlatsi Mango Shop/Cultivars – Hoedspruit Limpopo, South Africa. I had the pleasure of gaining some knowledge into the world of mangoes by getting a tour of the facility by Jaco. He is a walking encyclopedia when it comes to mangoes and I absolutely love learning new things.

1.Jaco Fivaz, farm manager of Mohlatsi farm in Limpopo, is a pioneer of high-density mango orchards, which achieve a greater yield per hectare than conventional orchards. Hoedspruit is a great area to have an orchard due to the long, warm, humid, wet summers which is an ideal growing climate for mangoes.

2.They are currently running one of the largest cultivar and selection evaluation programs in the Southern Hemisphere. They are the biggest breeding program that has over 800 seedlings and trying to see what works best for the business.

3.There are an astonishing 1900 cultivars in the world.

4.Their packhouse employs 75 full time employees, and during the harvest seasons, they double their employees. There are 100 employees that are dedicated to pruning the orchards. In the drying facility, there are 100 workers; 20 are permanent workers.

5.They have a farm stall on the farm that sells direct from the fields, so you can find fresh mangoes, as well as plenty other treats to eat that they produce from the farm. You can find Jaco's wife Belinda in the shop, and she is a cheerful face to welcome you.

Trees in blossom

Varieties

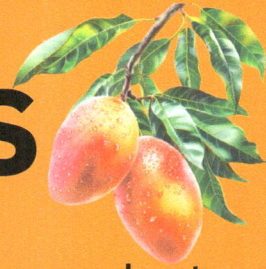

There are some popular varieties here. Let me tell you the most popular. Maybe you have tasted some of these before.

1. SENSATION
Originated in India

2. TOMMY ATKINS, KEIT, KENT
Originated in Florida

3. JOA, PRINCESS
Originated in South Africa

4. SHELLY
Originated in Israel

My *favorite*

5. LORMEY
Originated in South Africa – Cultivars Mohlatsi

It Takes *Two* to Mango

Kent mango is rated best eating mango in the world.

They are very sweet and fibreless.

Check at your local grocery store to see what variety you have.

All in the taste

<u>Lormey</u> (my favorite)
has a tropical taste and hints
of coconut and peach.

<u>Shelly</u> is sweet
and extremely juicy.

<u>Keit</u> has nutty/pecan
notes in it's flavor.

<u>Tommy Atkins</u> is a bit more
bland in flavor – my opinion.

To the orchard

Did you know that each mango must be picked by hand, and no big machinery is used?
The workers you will see, are picking each mango and setting them into specialized crates.
Then a tractor comes to collect them to transport them carefully into the packhouse for inspection.

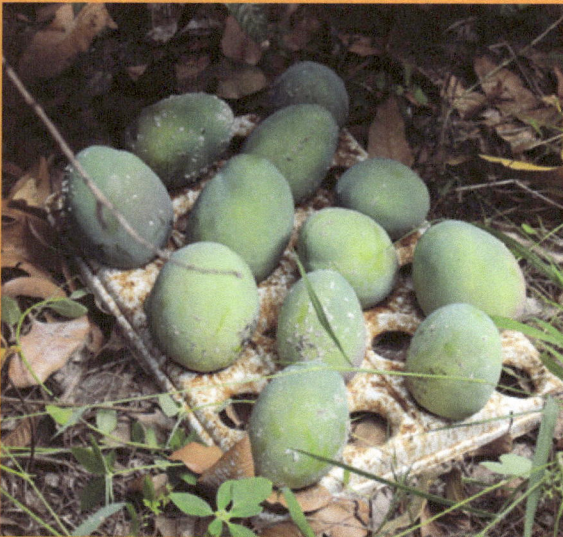

They are placed cut stem side down, as there are juices that come from the mangoes cut stem, that can burn the flesh. They sit in these trays for 20 minutes to 1hour. **IT** can also irritate your skin.

When the drip time has passed, the workers load them all by hand into large bins on the tractor.

Pruning usually happens from October – December, and post-harvest. You must prune trees to achieve high yields.

Problems

BUGS
If trees are too dense, you will sometimes find many mealy bugs.

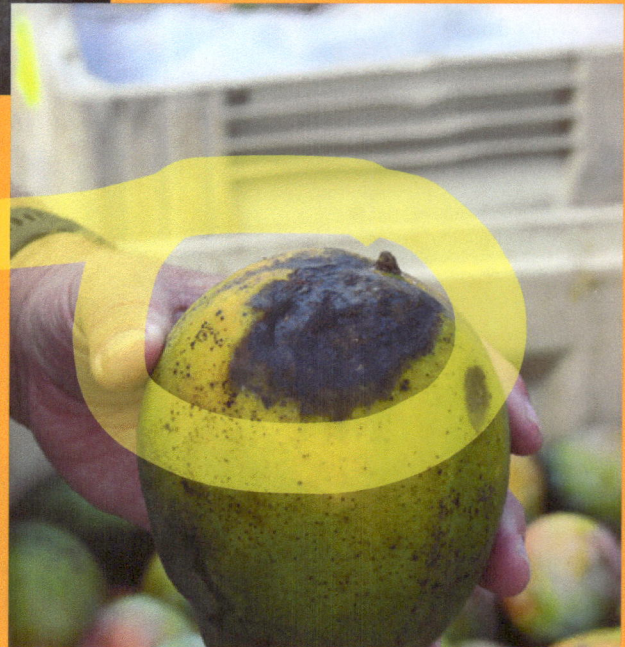

SUNBURN
Yes, a mango can also get sunburn....

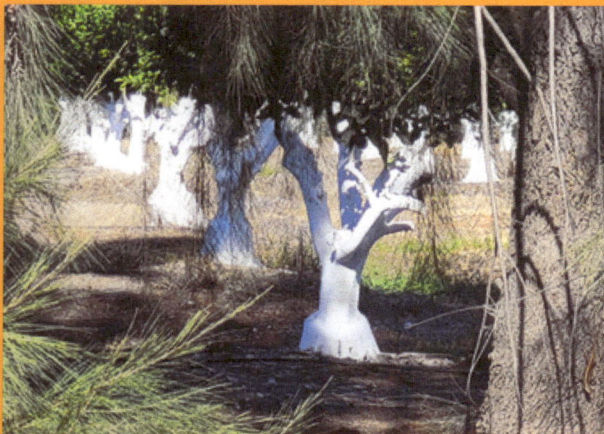

The stems get painted white to avoid sunburn

STEPS INVOLVED

LET'S NOW LOOK AT THE STEPS INVOLVED AFTER THEY LEAVE THE FIELD.

WEIGHED
They get weighed in large bins.

DUMPED INTO A BATH
This first step is a food safe chlorine for sanitizing

SORTED
Leaves/debris are removed

BRUSHES
It passes multiple brushes on rollers that gently scrub them.

AIR
They pass on a conveyor belt past an airdryer

HEATED WATER
Now they pass through heated water about 48 degrees celcius

LET'S NOW LOOK AT THE STEPS INVOLVED AFTER THEY LEAVE THE FIELD.

3-5 MINUTES
They stay in this hot water for a few minutes. This extends their shelf life.

FUNGICIDE
They go through a bath of fungicide.

AIR
More quick air drying

POLISH TIME
Now time for them to shine! Wax polish is used. Plastic wax makes them shiny and they look inviting.

SHELLAC WAX IS NOT USED
Shellac wax is actually secrection of the female lac bug...their poop, it looks dull. Doesn't travel well. It takes about 100,000 lac bugs to make 1 pound (0.4kg) of shellac resin.

NOW FOR SORTING

The artificial wax is food grade safe.

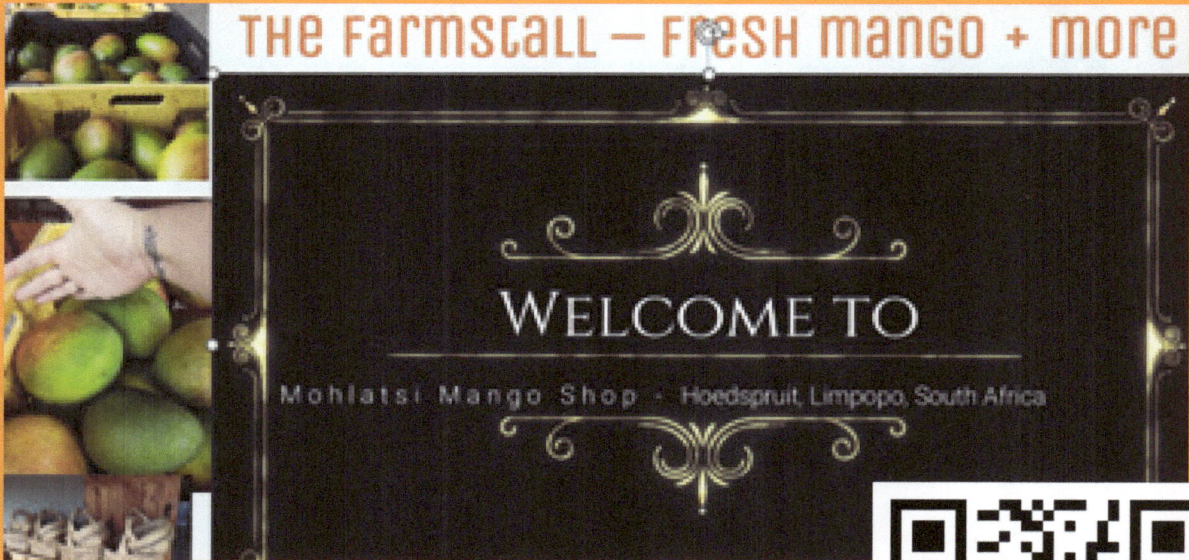
THE FARMSTALL — FRESH MANGO + MORE

WELCOME TO

Mohlatsi Mango Shop · Hoedspruit, Limpopo, South Africa

Scan to watch the full video of the process the mangoes go through

This hi-tech maching has weighed so far 11 million mangos.
It can weigh to pack 4,600 mangos/hr.
It weighs each fruit seperately.

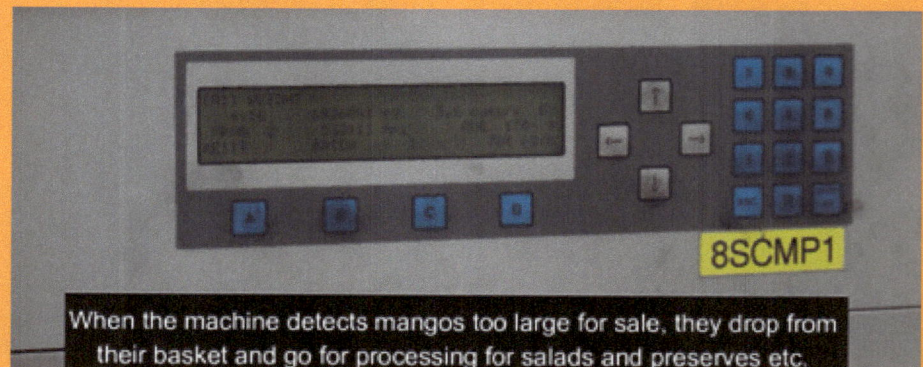
8SCMP1

When the machine detects mangos too large for sale, they drop from their basket and go for processing for salads and preserves etc.

Nice and shiny

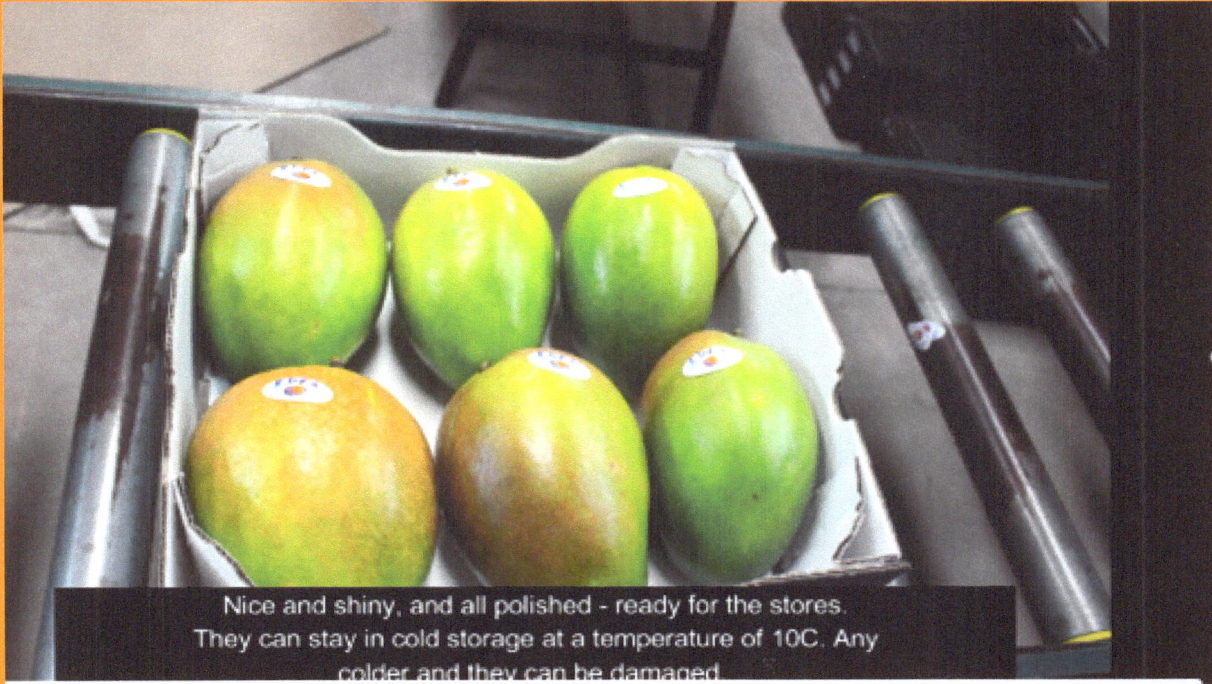

Nice and shiny, and all polished - ready for the stores.
They can stay in cold storage at a temperature of 10C. Any
colder and they can be damaged.

LEAVES TELL ALL

WHAT'S IN A LEAF?

Of course the farmer of the various cultivars are experts when it comes to identification. Could you tell the differences?

Scan the QR to see the video inside the mango shop - lots of sweet treats.

Part 2 - Dried Mango

How do we get to this stage?

THE MANGO SORTING

- In the facility, the mangoes all need to be sorted. They will look for the ones that are too large, have blemishes like sunburn, and bug bites, etc, and deem those ones non-marketable. Perfect for eating still, just don't look as good in their appearance for the supermarket shelves.

Nets will cover the sorted bins to prevent further damage like the hot mid-day African sun!

interesting facts!

1
BINS
24 bins/day are sorted

2
WEIGHT
Each bin weighs 400kg

3
process room
4 workers/table

It only takes the workers about 20 seconds or less to peel and cut 1 mango!

4
Quantity
Those 4 workers peel/cut +/-1.6 tonnes daily (3527.4 pounds)

5
impressive!
They go through 80 crates per day cutting and peeling our favorite dried treat!

Time yourself the next time you are peeling a carrot, potato, apple, or mango, and see how long it takes you.

The workers in the first stage

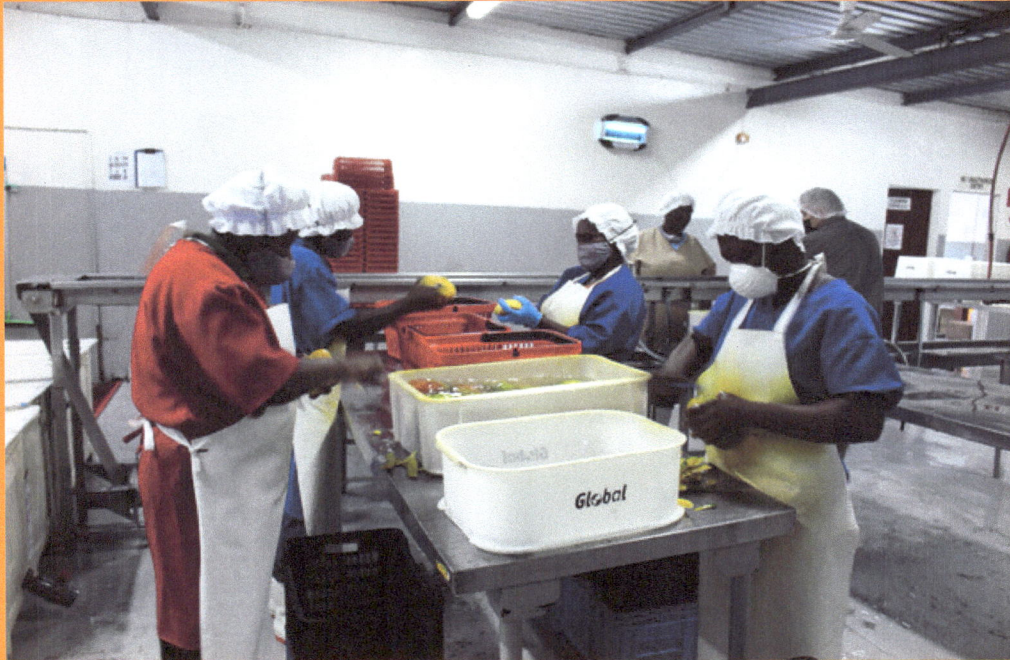

These workers are fast, efficient, and dedicated to their job. They are quite fascinating to watch how effortlessly, they can peel and slice mango. Getting to this level would take me many years! Those knives are SHARP.

Perfect peeling!

Scan to watch the video of this magical process

Now for a ride on the conveyor belt... to the cutting end

One by one, a worker stands by to assist each basket.

Once the mangoes fall into these baskets, they roll onto the next step.

With each green basket, now they need to go through a "wash process" which is a spray with sodium metabisulfate which = preserve. There is 1.6kg of "preserve" in 100litre of H2O.

1. Baskets go into the spray bath along rollers.

2. This process takes 2 minutes, and workers inside this stage ensure all mangoes get coated.

3. There is also a process in which they will do testing to ensure they have the correct sulphur preserve ratios and there is a lab within the facility to do frequent testing on each batch. They want to ensure the proper ratios to have adequate shelf life. Prime parts per million will normally range 300-400ppm , but sometimes sweeter mango varieties like Kent, will range around 110 parts per million.

I am standing outside of this area for protection. The sulphur smell is very strong and one needs time to get used to this.

Next steps before the ovens

Workers lay them in a single layer on trays.

Scan to watch this next process

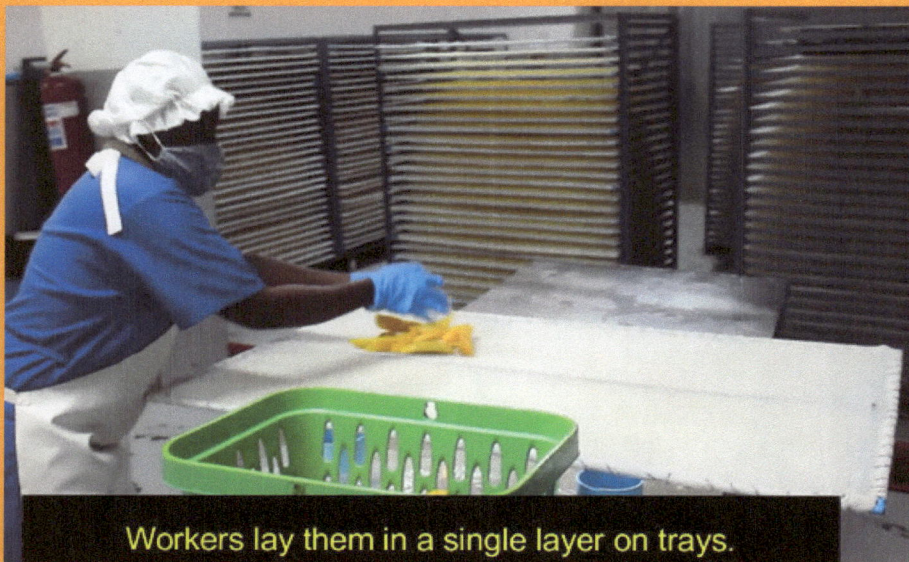

These "trays" are mesh nets

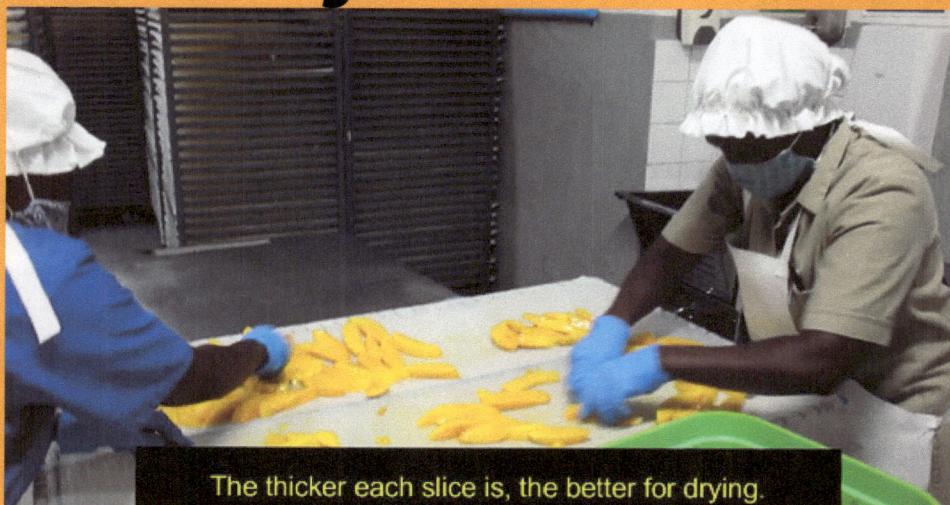

The thicker each slice is, the better for drying.

Looking great!

They look great and smell great too, but at this stage, you cannot eat them. The high levels of the chemical sulphur would make you very ill, and likely vomit very quickly.

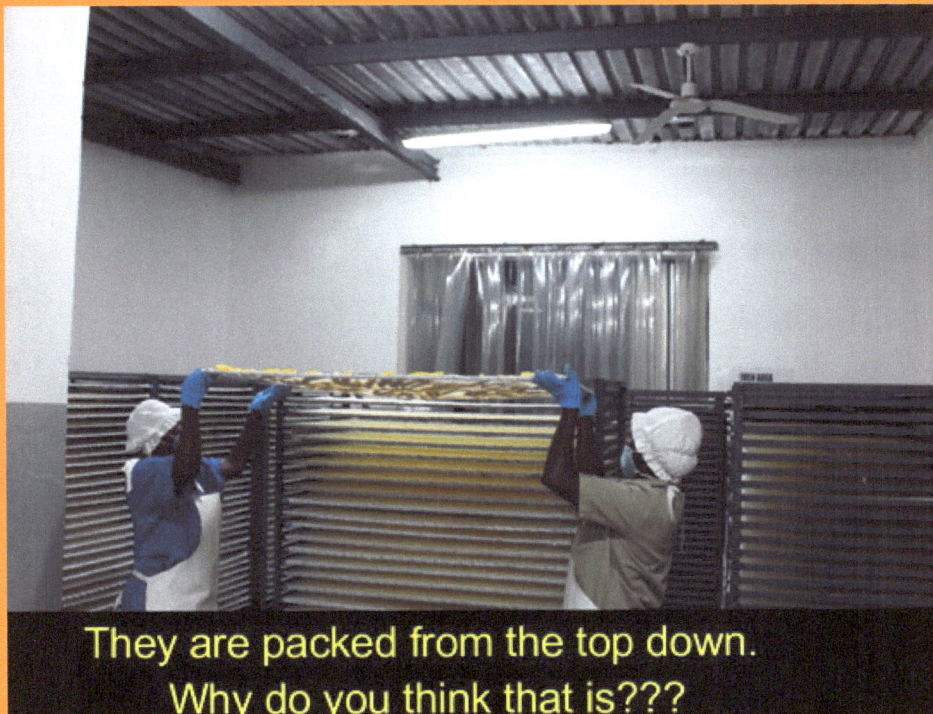

They are packed from the top down. Why do you think that is???

A: Too avoid the trays from getting too saturated by the other trays drippings.

NOW THAT THEY HAVE BEEN SORTED FOR THE OVEN.....A FEW FACTS...

OVENS

Each oven can dry 2 tonnes of wet mango

HOW HOT IS THE OVEN?

It is 59 degrees celcius!

HOW MANY OVENS?

There are 3 ovens

HOW MANY TRAYS?

In each oven, it can hold 10 trollies!

DURATION

It takes <u>17 hours </u>in the oven to dry each mangoes batch.

CALCULATIONS

Each oven needs a specific amount of humidity, heat, and time.

LET'S NOW LOOK AT THE OVENS INVOLVED

There are trays in the oven ready to go....

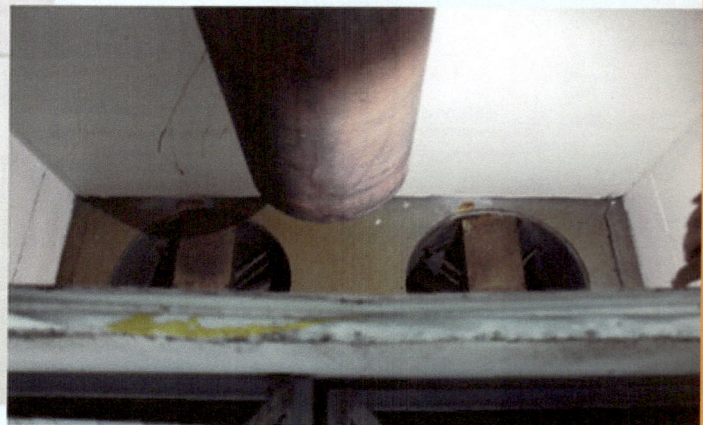

When water in the radiator is heated, the surrounding air is also heated up via convection and this hot air is then moved around the space as the air circulates.

LET'S LOOK AT THE OVEN CONTROL

It is quite amazing that the oven is so controlled to ensure the mango are dried to perfection. This is a science that has taken many years to prefect the perfect drying steps and every country will have their own process.

The control on the oven tells the computer how long to cook at each temperature and what humidity along the process.

AND ONCE THE MANGO HAVE SPENT THEIR TIME IN THE OVEN... THE NEXT STEPS..

- They will go to the next sorting phase.

  - Workers will be very maticulous here.

  - They are the quality control/hands on

  - These workers ensure **each and every**

  piece is suitable for eating.

  - They must follow regulations and discard pieces that

  contain spots, burn, and use sissors to trim sharp or jagged edges.

LOOK AT THE WORKERS IN THE FINAL STAGE

WHAT HAPPENS HERE

Workers inspect each and every piece of dried mango.
When I say each, I mean every single piece!
They must inspect each piece and hand cut off sharp edges, dark or white spots, and discard anything not suitable in appearance. They do this BY HAND!

once inspected

The dried mango pieces all go into bags for boxing.

But WAIT.... There's more.....

each box...

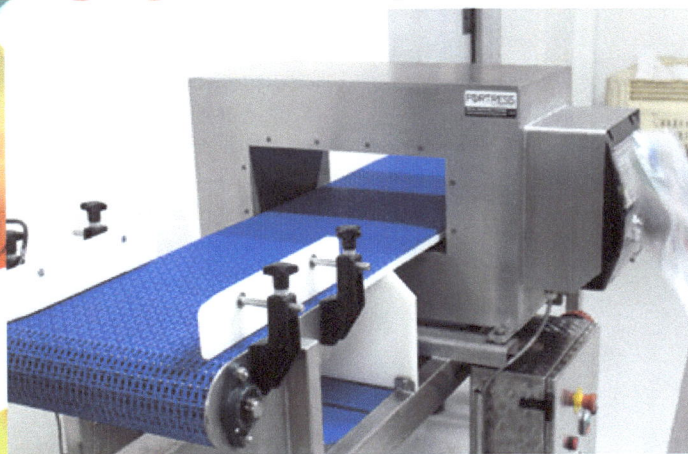

Needs to pass through the metal detector to ensure NO METAL Is found in the boxes.

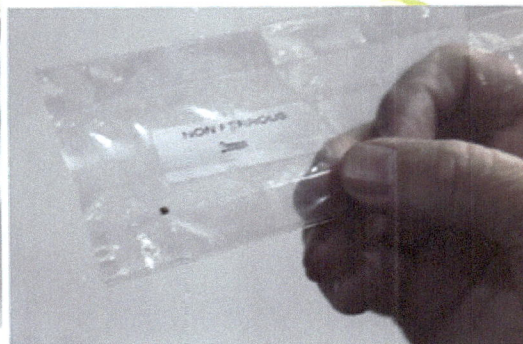

Each and every single crate and bag of dried mangoes will pass through this scanner for metal. Even the tiniest piece will be detected like I watched the example of this small piece above, and it set the loud alarm off immediately.

NOW WHaT?

The boxes are all marked with a special number and this number shows us many things like the date it was packed, who was working that day, the driver etc.

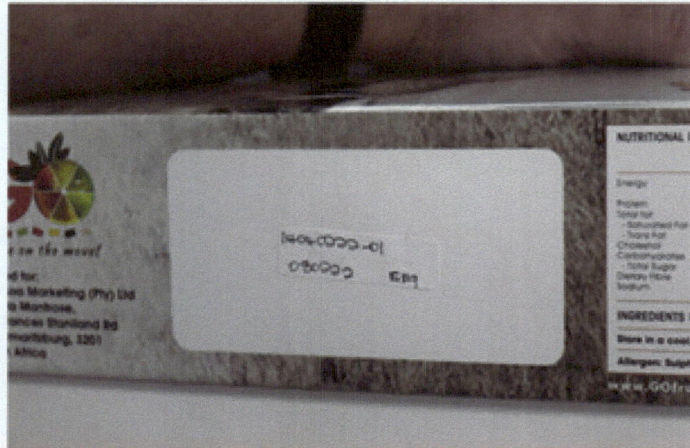

WHere In THe WORLD?

These mangoes will be going on a journey to local stores in South Africa, Japan and the Netherlands.

Now you see what lengths a mango goes through from orchard to supermarket

ARE YOU GETTING HUNGRY YET?

ORANGES

Chapter 2

Oranges

are delicious anytime

I bet you can almost smell this picture.

Now we will learn about the journey the oranges take from the orchard to the markets. Let's go!

Scan for the intro video

Follow me on my learning day at Unifrutti Packhouse

Located in the heart of the Lowveld, Unifrutti has built a unique offer, characterized by variety, quality, and flexibility thanks to the global extent of it's inclusive and integrated business model and by directly owning and supervising 14,000 hectares (that's almost 35,000 acres) of farms.

Unifrutti's product standards are nothing but excellence. To guarantee customers the product they deserve, the Group has always considered the highest quality of fruit as its average product level. Being committed to offering the best quality fresh fruit every day, in any season, means following the strictest global guidelines and reaching the highest efficiency in production. Regardless of the season or the production location, Unifrutti applies the same rules and the same supply chain controls, in order to produce in the most efficient and sustainable way, respecting workers and the environment. Because quality to us also means providing a better quality of life to everyone. They run quality controls daily on EVERY shipment that leaves the packhouse!

Big thanks to Don Coetzee of Unifrutti for taking time from his day, to take me through the orchard and packhouse to show me this journey.

Driving to the Orchards

Hippopotamus

Sometimes there are hippos here that mow the grass for free each night.

The workers
use ladders
to reach the top.

Look at all those
beautiful oranges.
Every
orange is hand picked.

Each worker,
(men & women)
has a sling bag, and
they
have a pair of clippers
that they cut each
orange with. They put
the oranges in their
sling bag until it
is full.
Once it is full, they
race
back to the tractor
to empty the bag,
and race back to the
tree to fill it again.
They do this all day.

Natalie Chiassón Weyers

They then will "clock in" each bag that is
counted for them to know how many each
picker has picked. A daily quota must be met
for fair pay.

VERY IMPORTANT:

Any stems are then cut
short if missed so, they don't
damage other fruit in the
transporting to the
packhouse.

These workers amaze me at their speed.
They are not chatting to each other. They
are fast at work.
I know I could not do this at the same
speed at they are going.

Here are two videos of the workers in the
orchards picking the oranges.

The pickers are fast!
The tractor bins fill quickly.

Each bin can hold 2 tonnes. That is 2000kg/4400 pounds

Any that spill onto the ground are unusable.
They get put into a pile to keep fruit flies away from the trees, and then chopped up.

What a view!

Here they arrive at the packhouse...Let us see the process here...

Scan the QR to play video

They go up
the conveyor.

They get a
gentle scrub.

These workers
assess the
quality.

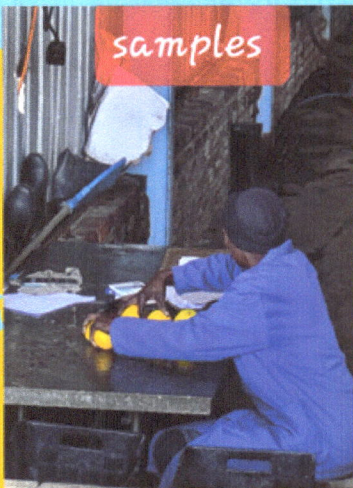

samples

She checks for bugs, marks,
moth damage, scars, fruit fly,
wind damage, oversize and
undersize fruits.

This lady takes
samples from
each bin.

She keeps a log tally
from every bin.

39

NEXT STEPS:

They take a warm 35C bath quickly, then they get a fungicide spray, go through a dryer, get gentle brushing, get a coat of wax, then another dryer, then prepare for final grading system.

Scan QR to PLAY

I wish you could scratch and sniff to smell the aroma in the packhouse.

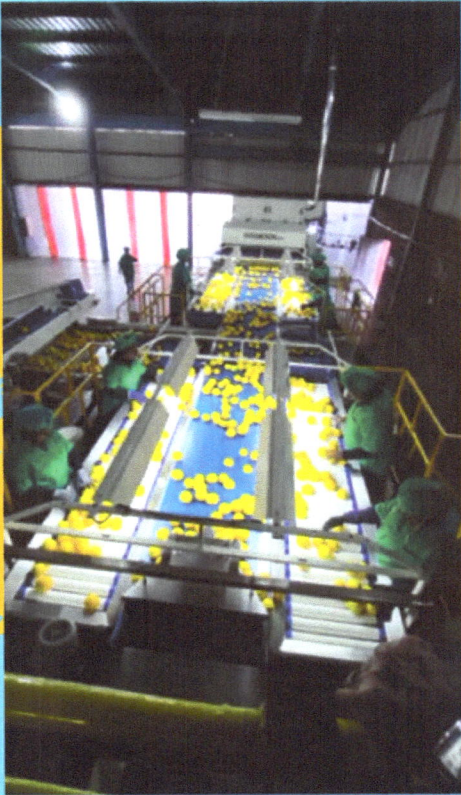

The workers here will do a final grading on the oranges. They check each orange and ensure they are all the highest quality before going onward with
their journey.

Scan QR to watch along

These workers are fast at sorting

THE HIGH TECH CAMERA

This camera takes 21 pictures of each fruit as it passes on the belt. This camera is on a 6 lane conveyor that gets all angles of the fruit. It can detect quality, size, etc. Scan QR to watch it in action.

It is continuously flashing taking all the pictures of the oranges.

THE HIGH TECH CAMERA

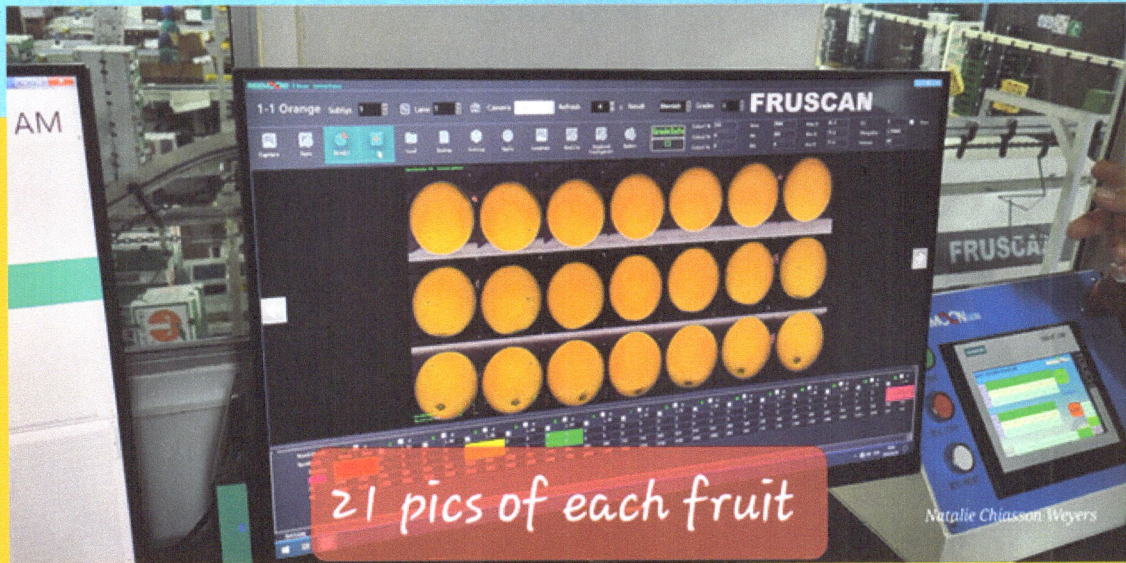

21 pics of each fruit

Natalie Chiasson Weyers

Now that is what I call a good CAMERA! The journey doesn't stop here. Watch next, how the conveyor knows to toss oranges that are not in the Class 1 or 2. All class 3 goes to juicing facility.

Say Cheese

IT DETECTS FOR ANY
CLASS 3- THEN THIS IS THEIR
FINAL STOP, POP, AND OFF
THEY GO.
Watch them popping. Those will
go to the juicing factory. These are
not good
for export as they're lower quality.
They fall down to the bottom
where they are boxed for the juice
factory.

Only the Class 1 & 2 - the prime
highest quality get exported.
Scan QR to watch along

This facility exports internationally
to China, Hong Kong, UK, India, Malaysia, Russia etc.

HOW

COOL

In a 9hour shift, there are 180 tonnes of oranges processed -
A whopping 180,000kg which is 396,000 pounds!

In a season, January - end of August,
1.3 million cartons are packed.
The packhouse employes 130 seasonal workers per packhouse which locally there are 2, so that is 260 seasonal workers

JOB

Jobs for many people

Last look at the fruit before the trucks arrive:

Boxes waiting to be filled.

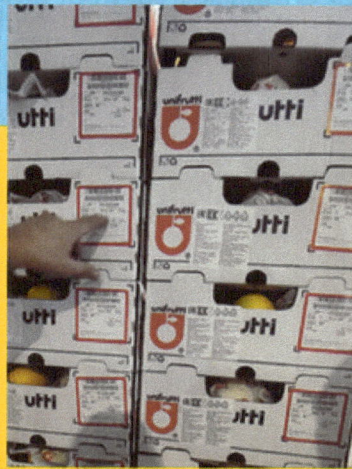

Each label shows date, where it's from, where it is headed, quality class, and how many per box.

Crates awaiting the truck.

Each day, once the fruit is picked and goes through the steps in the packhouse, then:

The full boxes go onto large crate pallets, transports collect 25-28 pallets each day for delivery to the harbors to export to ensure quality and freshness.

The biggest running costs are:

- **Labor costs**
- **Packaging materials**
- **Transportation**

Once oranges and mangoes leave the factory, they starts the journey via transport trucks and cargo ships, to the supermarkets. That is where you can now buy some delicious oranges for snacks and baking.

 Transports

Cargo ships

All the rejected class 3 fruit head to the juicing factory. And, the cattle also get a treat!

MOOO

Tips & Uses for Mango and Orange

Here are the benefits of eating **<u>mangoes</u>**, explained in a kid-friendly way:

1. Vitamin C Power: Mangoes are full of vitamin C, which helps keep you from getting sick.
2. Yummy Fiber: The fiber in mangoes helps your tummy stay happy and healthy.
3. Germ Fighters: Mangoes have special things called antioxidants that help fight off germs and keep you strong.
4. Heart Helper: Eating mangoes helps keep your heart healthy and your blood pressure just right.
5. Hydration Station: Mangoes are juicy and help keep you hydrated.
6. Glow Up: The vitamins in mangoes help your skin stay smooth and shiny.
7. Eye Protectors: Mangoes have vitamins that keep your eyes healthy and help you see better.
8. Energy Boost: Mangoes help your body absorb iron from other foods, giving you more energy.
9. Healthy Treat: Mangoes are low in calories, so you can eat them as a sweet and healthy snack.

Here are the benefits of eating **oranges**, explained in a kid-friendly way:

1. Super Vitamin C: Oranges are packed with vitamin C, which helps keep you from getting sick.
2. Tummy Helper: The fiber in oranges helps your tummy stay happy and healthy.
3. Fights Germs: Oranges have special things called antioxidants that help fight off germs and keep you strong.
4. Heart Hero: Eating oranges helps keep your heart healthy and your blood pressure just right.
5. Thirst Quencher: Oranges are juicy and help keep you hydrated.
6. Glowing Skin: The vitamin C in oranges helps your skin stay smooth and shiny.
7. Bright Eyes: Oranges have vitamins that keep your eyes healthy and help you see better.
8. Iron Boost: Oranges help your body absorb iron from other foods, giving you more energy. They are also low in calories.

Fun ways to eat Mango

Mangoes:
1. Mango Cubes: Cut a mango into cubes and eat them with a fork or toothpick for a fun, bite-sized snack.
2. Mango Popsicles: Puree mango in a blender and pour it into popsicle molds to freeze for a sweet, cold treat.
3. Mango Smoothies: Blend mango chunks with milk or yogurt and a little honey for a delicious smoothie.
4. Mango on a Stick: Peel a mango, slice it into chunks, and stick them on a skewer for a fun, portable snack.
5. Mango Salsa: Mix mango cubes with a bit of lime juice, chopped red bell pepper, and a pinch of salt for a tasty salsa to eat with tortilla chips.

Fun ways to eat Oranges

Oranges:
1. Orange Smiles: Peel an orange and separate the segments. Arrange them like a smiley face on a plate for a fun and healthy snack.
2. Orange Popsicles: Squeeze fresh orange juice into popsicle molds and freeze for a refreshing treat.
3. Fruit Salad: Mix orange segments with other fruits like grapes, apples, and bananas for a colorful fruit salad.
4. Orange Smoothies: Blend orange juice with yogurt and a banana for a creamy and delicious smoothie.
5. Orange Slices with Cinnamon: Sprinkle a little cinnamon on orange slices for a tasty twist.

Choosing the perfect MANGO

Here are some tips for picking the ripest mango at the supermarket:

1. Color: While the color of a mango can vary depending on the variety, generally look for mangoes with vibrant hues of red, yellow, or orange. Green patches are fine as long as the mango has some color development.
2. Squeeze Test: Gently squeeze the mango. A ripe mango will give slightly under pressure, similar to a ripe peach or avocado. Avoid mangoes that are too hard or too mushy.
3. Smell: Smell the stem end of the mango. A ripe mango will have a sweet, fruity aroma. If there's no smell, it might not be ripe yet.
4. Texture: The skin of a ripe mango may have some wrinkles and feel slightly soft, but it should not have large dark spots or feel too squishy.

Shape: Choose mangoes that are plump and rounded. Avoid shriveled skin, as they might be overripe or have poor texture.

Choosing the best ORANGE

1. Weight: Pick up the orange and feel its weight. A good, juicy orange will feel heavy for its size. This indicates that it's full of juice.
2. Texture: Look for oranges with a smooth, firm skin. Avoid oranges with soft spots, blemishes, or wrinkled skin, as these can be signs of overripe or dry fruit.
3. Color: Choose oranges that have a bright, vibrant color. While a little bit of green can be okay, especially around the stem, the skin should generally be a rich orange hue. Avoid dull or faded-looking oranges.
4. Smell: Give the orange a sniff. A ripe, juicy orange will have a fresh, citrusy aroma. If there's no scent, it might not be ripe yet.
5. Skin Thickness: While not always easy to determine, oranges with thinner skin often have more juice. You can sometimes tell by gently squeezing the fruit—thin-skinned oranges will have a bit more give.

Can we eat the peelings???

Yes, you can eat **orange peel**, but there are a few things to keep in mind:

1. Nutritional Benefits: Orange peels are rich in fiber, vitamins, and antioxidants. They contain higher amounts of certain nutrients, like vitamin C and flavonoids, compared to the flesh.
2. Taste and Texture: The peel is quite bitter and tough compared to the sweet and juicy flesh of the orange. This can make it less palatable to eat raw.
3. Pesticides: Orange skins may contain pesticide residues. If you plan to eat the peel, it's best to choose organic oranges and wash them thoroughly to remove any chemicals.
4. Culinary Uses: Orange zest (the outermost layer of the peel) is often used in cooking and baking to add a burst of citrus flavor. The white part of the peel (pith) is more bitter and less commonly used.
5. Health Considerations: While eating small amounts of orange peel can be beneficial, consuming large quantities might cause digestive discomfort due to its high fiber content.

Many people prefer to use orange peel in recipes rather than eating it raw. It can be candied, grated for zest, or used to infuse flavors into dishes and beverages.

Yes, you can eat **mango peel** too, but there are several factors to consider:

1. Nutritional Benefits: Mango peels are rich in fiber, vitamins, antioxidants, and other beneficial compounds.
2. Taste and Texture: Mango peels have a tough, chewy texture and a slightly bitter taste, which some people may find unpleasant.
3. Urushiol Content: Mango peels contain urushiol, a compound also found in poison ivy and poison oak, which can cause allergic reactions in some people. If you're sensitive to urushiol, it's best to avoid eating mango peels.
4. Pesticides: As with many fruits, mango skins may have pesticide residues. If you decide to eat the peel, choose organic mangoes and wash them thoroughly.
5. Culinary Uses: Instead of eating mango peel directly, you can use it in recipes where it can be blended or cooked to reduce its bitterness and toughness. For example, it can be added to smoothies or used to make jams and chutneys.

While it is safe for most people to eat mango peel, individual preferences and sensitivities vary. If you decide to try it, start with a small amount to see how your body reacts.

What snack

are you choosing?

The end

I am an online teacher. I teach ESL, as well as about animals, bugs, creatures, and critters.

I mainly write my stories so I can teach my students about some interesting things in South Africa. This book is what I have also created one of my classes around and my students love it!

If you want to find more of my books on Amazon, type Mrs Natalie Chiasson in the search bar. I have books about animals, as well as books for your children to practice their reading. Thanks for your support. Scan the QR to find me on Outschool.

I have many books, journals, composition notebooks, calendars, etc listed on Amazon. Search my name Mrs Natalie Chiasson

or Amazon.ca scan here

Some of my listings

Ding, Dong, Dung: A Book About Poop From Animals in South Africa

Upside-Down Roots of Resilience: Majestic Baobab Trees of South Africa

Birthday Tracker
by Mrs Natalie Chiasson
Paperback

My Health Matters To Me: Daily Logbook
by Mrs Natalie Chiasson

Life's Big Journeys - Wise Words With Animals: Bedtime Stories

Katherine's Chocolate Adventure in Candy Land
by Mrs Natalie Chiasson

Winter Whispers and Snowflake Wishes
by Mrs Natalie Chiasson

Day Planner
by Mrs Natalie Chiasson
★★★★★ ✓ 1

If Zebras Could Talk, the Tales They Would Tell
by Mrs Natalie Chiasson

My Safari of Animals, Creatures, & Critters of South Africa: Book 1

Gap Year: Tips, Travel Hacks, & Planner
by Mrs Natalie Chiasson

A Birthday Wish: I Can Read
by Mrs Natalie Chiasson
★★★★☆ ✓ 1

A Book for Year End Signatures: & Notes from Your Friends

Daily Tracker
by Mrs Natalie Chiasson
Paperback

Mark It Down Before You Forget
by Mrs Natalie Chiasson

Special thanks to Jaco Fivaz & Don Coetzee for proofing my information to ensure it is accurate before submission. 2024

The end